The Dawning *of* Indestructible Joy

DAILY READINGS FOR ADVENT

JOHN PIPER

 **CROSSWAY**

WHEATON, ILLINOIS

The Dawning of Indestructible Joy: Daily Readings for Advent

Copyright © 2014 by Desiring God Foundation

Published by Crossway
1300 Crescent Street
Wheaton, Illinois 60187

Cover design: Erik Maldre

Cover image: The Bridgeman Art Library

First printing 2014

Printed in the United States of America

Unless otherwise indicated, Scripture quotations are from the ESV® Bible (*The Holy Bible, English Standard Version®*), copyright © 2001 by Crossway. 2011 Text Edition. Used by permission. All rights reserved.

Scripture quotations marked KJV are from the *King James Version* of the Bible.

Scripture quotations marked NASB are from *The New American Standard Bible®*. Copyright © The Lockman Foundation 1960, 1962, 1963, 1968, 1971, 1972, 1973, 1975, 1977, 1995. Used by permission.

Scripture quotations marked NIV are taken from The Holy Bible, New International Version®, NIV®. Copyright © 1973, 1978, 1984, 2011 by Biblica, Inc.™ Used by permission. All rights reserved worldwide.

All emphases in Scripture quotations have been added by the author.

Trade paperback ISBN: 978-1-4335-4236-7
ePub ISBN: 978-1-4335-4239-8
PDF ISBN: 978-1-4335-4237-4
Mobipocket ISBN: 978-1-4335-4238-1

Library of Congress Cataloging-in-Publication Data

Piper, John, 1946-
  [Meditations. Selections]
  The Dawning of indestructible joy : daily readings for
Advent / John Piper.
    pages cm
  ISBN 978-1-4335-4236-7 (tp)
  1. Advent—Meditations. 2. Bible. New Testament—
Devotional use. I. Title.
BV40.P53   2014
242'.332—dc23   2014007719

Crossway is a publishing ministry of Good News Publishers.

LB		24	23	22	21	20	19	18	17	16	15	14
15	14	13	12	11	10	9	8	7	6	5	4	3	2	1

To Sam Storms,
comrade in Christian Hedonism,
precious friend for indestructible joy.

Contents

Preface

I feel like the apostle Peter at the end of his life, as he wrote his second letter. Twice he told his readers why he was writing to them. In the first chapter he said, "I think it right, as long as I am in this body, to stir you up by way of reminder" (2 Pet. 1:13). Then, in the last chapter, he said it again: "I am stirring up your sincere mind by way of reminder" (2 Pet. 3:1).

His aim was first to remind them. And then, by reminding them, to stir them up. That's what this little book of Advent devotional readings is for—reminders and stirrings.

The Greek word for "stir up" is used most often for waking someone from sleep. That's the way it's used, for example, in Mark 4:39: "[Jesus] *awoke* and rebuked the wind." Peter assumes that his Christian readers need to be wakened. I know I continually need awakening. Especially when Christmas approaches.

I am prone to be dull, spiritually drowsy, halfhearted, lukewarm. That is the way human beings are, including Christians, even about great things. Peter knows it and is writing to "awaken" or to "stir up" his readers so that they don't just know but also feel the wonder of the truth.

That's why I have written these devotions. What you and I need is usually not a brand-new teaching. Brand-new truths are probably not truths. What we need are reminders about the greatness of the old truths. We need someone to say an old truth in a fresh way. Or sometimes, just to say it.

What Peter really means, and what I mean, by being "awakened" or "stirred up" is to feel some measure of the joy God intends for Christmas to bring. "Behold, I bring you good news of great joy" (Luke 2:10). Not small joy. Not modest joy. But "great joy." If we don't feel this when we ponder the incarnation of the Son of God, we need "awakening." We need to be "stirred up."

I have called Christmas—and this little book—"the dawning of indestructible joy" because the joy Jesus was bringing into the world was like no other kind in history. Once we have it, it cannot be destroyed. Jesus said, "No one will take your joy from you" (John 16:22).

The joy that Jesus came to bring is from outside this world. It is the very joy that Jesus himself has in God the Father—which he has had from all eternity and will have forever. There is no greater joy than the joy that God has in God, because God is the greatest object of joy, and God has the greatest powers to enjoy.

Jesus said, "I have spoken to you, that *my joy* may be in you, and that your joy may be full" (John 15:11). His joy was the very joy of God. He promises to put that in us. That is what the Holy Spirit does. He pours out the love of God in our hearts (Rom. 5:5), and with it the joy of God in God. "The fruit of the Spirit is love, joy . . ." (Gal. 5:22). This is "great joy." And it cannot be taken away. It is indestructible.

Ah, but it can go to sleep. That's why Peter says, "I think it right, as long as I am in this body, to stir you up by way of reminder" (2 Pet. 1:13). Yes. It is very right. Because, oh, how wrong, how sad, when we stand before great wonders and feel nothing. It is right, therefore, that he write and I write to awaken and stir up our affections for the greatest wonder of all: the arrival and the work and the person of Jesus Christ, the Son of God, in this world.

May the Spirit of God use these words to open your eyes afresh to the glories of Christ and give you a new taste of your indestructible joy.

Praying for Fullness This Christmas

The Word became flesh and dwelt among us, and we have seen his glory, glory as of the only Son from the Father, full of grace and truth. . . . For *from his fullness we have all received, grace upon grace.*

JOHN 1:14–16

It was a drenching moment for me that Advent. A man in our church had just prayed the words of John 1:14–16 in a pre-service prayer meeting. God granted me in that moment that the word "fullness" fill me. It was an extraordinary experience. There was a kind of Holy Spirit soaking.

I felt some measure of what the word really carries—*the fullness of Christ*. I felt some of the wonder that I had indeed received grace upon grace from this fullness. And I was at that moment receiving grace upon grace. I felt right then that nothing would have been sweeter than to simply sit at his feet—or read my Bible—all afternoon and feel his fullness overflow.

Why did this fullness have such an impact on me—and why is it still to this moment affecting me unusually? In part because:

- the one from whose fullness I am being drenched with grace is the *Word* that was with God and *was God* (John 1:1–2), so that his fullness is the fullness of God—a *divine fullness, an infinite fullness*;
- this Word became flesh and so was one of us and was pursuing us with his fullness—so it is an *accessible fullness*;
- when this Word appeared in human form, his *glory* was seen—his is a *glorious fullness*;
- this Word was "the only Son from the Father" so that the divine fullness was being mediated to me not just from God but through God—God did not send an angel but *his only Son to deliver his fullness*;
- the fullness of the Son is a fullness of grace—I will not drown in this fullness but be *blessed in every way by this fullness*;
- this fullness is not only a fullness of grace but also of truth—I am not being graced with truth-ignoring flattery; *this grace is rooted in rock-solid reality.*

As I savor this illumination of Christ's fullness, I hear Paul say, "In him *the whole fullness of deity* dwells bodily" (Col. 2:9). I hear him say, "In him all *the fullness of God* was pleased to dwell" (Col. 1:19). And again, "In him are hidden *all the treasures* of wisdom and knowledge" (Col. 2:3).

Paul prays that we would *experience* Christ's fullness—not just know about it, but be filled with it. Here is the way I hear him praying for me: he prays that I "may have strength to comprehend with all the saints what is the breadth and length and height and depth, and to know the love of Christ that surpasses knowledge, that [I] may be filled with all the *fullness of God*" (Eph. 3:18–19).

The "fullness of God" is *experienced*, he says, as we are given the "strength to comprehend" the love of Christ in its height and depth and length and breadth. That is, in its *fullness*. This is remarkable: the fullness of God is the spiritual comprehension (experience) of the fullness of the love of Christ. It fills the Son of God and pours out on us.

So when I hear Paul speak to the Romans of "the fullness of the blessing of Christ" (Rom. 15:29), I hear him describing my experience. How I long for you all to know this.

Give yourself time and quietness in this Advent season and seek this experience. Pray for yourself the prayer of Paul in Ephesians 3:14–19—"that you may be filled with all the fullness of God"—that you may have power "to comprehend with all the saints what is the breadth and length and height and depth, and to know the love of Christ that surpasses knowledge."

That is my prayer for you this Christmas—that you would experience the fullness of Christ; that you would know in your heart the outpouring of grace upon grace; that the glory of the only Son from the Father would shine into your heart to give the light of the knowledge of the glory of God in the face of Christ; that you would be amazed that Christ can be so real to you.

The Search-and-Save Mission

The Son of Man came to seek and to save the lost.

LUKE 19:10

The word *advent* means "coming." In this season of the year, we focus on the meaning of the coming of the Son of God into the world. And the spirit of our celebration should be the spirit in which he came. And the spirit of that coming is summed up in Luke 19:10: "The Son of Man came to seek and to save the lost."

The coming of Jesus was a search-and-save mission. "The Son of Man came to seek and to save the lost."

So Advent is a season for thinking about the mission of God to seek and to save lost people from the wrath to come. God raised him from the dead, "Jesus who delivers us from the wrath to come" (1 Thess. 1:10). It's a season for cherishing and worshiping this characteristic of God—that he is a searching and saving God, that he is a God on a mission, that he is not aloof or passive or indecisive. He is never in the maintenance mode, coasting or drifting. He is sending, pursuing, searching, saving. That's the meaning of Advent.

The book of Acts is a celebration of this advent heart of God's—on the move to seek and to save the lost. It's a narration of Jesus's ongoing advent into more and more peoples of the world. Acts is the story of how the early church understood the words, "As the Father has sent me, even so I am sending you" (John 20:21). It's the story of how the vertical advent of God in the mission of Jesus bends out and becomes the horizontal advent of Jesus in the mission of the church. In us.

Jesus came into the world at the first Advent, and every Advent since is a reminder of his continual advent into more and more lives. And that advent is, in fact, our advent—our coming, our moving into the lives of those around us and into the peoples of the world.

Prepare Your Heart for Christ

How can you believe, when you receive glory from one another and do not seek the glory that comes from the only God?

JOHN 5:44

God owns and controls all things. And there is nothing that he could give you for Christmas this year that would suit your needs and your longings better than the consolation of Israel and the redemption of Jerusalem, restoration for past losses and liberation from future enemies, forgiveness and freedom, pardon and power, healing the past and sealing the future.

If there is a longing in your heart this Advent for something that the world has not been able to satisfy, might not this longing be God's Christmas gift preparing you to see Christ as consolation and redemption and to receive him for who he really is?

How is the heart prepared to receive Christ for who he really is? It is very simple.

First, the heart must become disenchanted with the praise of men. "How can you believe, when you receive glory from one another and do not seek the glory that comes from God?" (John 5:44; 7:17–18).

Second, the heart must become disenchanted with the sufficiency of money and things to satisfy the soul. "The Pharisees, who were lovers of money, heard all these things, and they ridiculed him" (Luke 16:14).

Then, third, alongside this disenchantment with the praise of men and the power of money, there must come into the heart a longing for consolation and a redemption beyond what the world can give.

Fourth and finally, there must be a revelation from God the Father, opening the eyes of the heart so that it cries out, like a man who stumbles onto an incredible treasure, "You are the Christ, the Son of the living God, the consolation of my past, the redemption of my future. Now I see you. Now I receive you—for who you really are."

May God do this for you this Advent. May this be your gift, and your witness, and the testimony of many this Advent.

Draw Near to the Savior

Now may the God of peace who brought again from the dead our Lord Jesus, the great shepherd of the sheep, by the blood of the eternal covenant, equip you with everything good that you may do his will, working in us that which is pleasing in his sight, through Jesus Christ, to whom be glory forever and ever. Amen.

HEBREWS 13:20–21

One of the things pleasing in God's sight is that his people keep on drawing near to him forever and ever. And so he is working in us this very thing.

Hebrews 13:21 says he is doing this "*through Jesus Christ,*" which means, at least, that Jesus has purchased this grace for us by his death and that Jesus prays and asks the Father for it on the basis of that death.

In other words, when the writer of Hebrews tells us that drawing near to God is what qualifies us for the eternal saving work of our High Priest, he doesn't mean to say that our High Priest leaves us alone in our sinful bent and natural resistance, as if we could draw near to God on our own. Rather, our High Priest intercedes for us and asks the Father to do just what Hebrews 13:21 says he will do—work in us what is pleasing in his sight—"through Jesus Christ."

Let me illustrate this by the way it looked when our High Priest was on the earth. In Luke 22:31–32 Jesus says to Peter, "Simon, Simon, behold, Satan demanded to have you, that he might sift you like wheat, but I have prayed for you that your faith may not fail. And when you have turned again, strengthen your brothers." So already Jesus was interceding for his own when he was on the earth. And he was praying that Peter's faith—*that his faith—our faith—not fail*.

Moreover, he was so confident in his prayer for Peter that he said, "*When* you have turned again," not, "*If* you turn again." So even though Peter stumbled in denial, his faith did not fail utterly. That is what the Lord prays for us. This is one more piece of our great security and hope in this great epistle of assurance.

Is it not a wonderful thing this Advent season to know that God bids us come? That this great, holy God of righteousness and wrath says, "Draw near to me through my Son, your High Priest. Draw near to me. *Draw near to me*"?

This is his invitation in these Advent readings: "Draw near to me through your High Priest. Draw near to me in confession and prayer and meditation and trust and praise. Come. I will not cast you out." For Christ "is able to save to the uttermost those who draw near to God through him, since he always lives to make intercession for them" (Heb. 7:25).

What Advent Is All About

Even the Son of Man came not to be served but to serve, and to give his life as a ransom for many.

MARK 10:45

Christmas is about the coming of Christ into the world. It's about the Son of God, who existed eternally with the Father as "the radiance of the glory of God and the exact imprint of his nature," taking on human nature and becoming man (Heb. 1:3).

It's about the virgin birth of a child conceived miraculously by the Holy Spirit so that he is the Son of God, not the way you and I are sons of God, but in an utterly unique way (Luke 1:35).

It's about the coming of a man named Jesus in whom "the whole fullness of deity dwells bodily" (Col. 2:9).

It's about the coming of the "fullness of time" that had been prophesied by the prophets of old that a ruler would be born in Bethlehem (Mic. 5:2); and a child would be born called

Wonderful Counselor, Mighty God, Everlasting Father, Prince of Peace (Isa. 9:6); and a Messiah, an anointed one, a shoot from the stem of Jesse, a Son of David, a King, would come (Isa. 11:1–4; Zech. 9:9).

And, according to Mark 10:45, Christmas is about the coming of the Son of Man who "came not to be served but to serve, and to give his life as a ransom for many." These words in Mark 10:45, as a brief expression of Christmas, are what I hope God will fix in your mind and heart this Advent.

Open your heart to receive the best present imaginable: *Jesus giving himself to die for you and to serve you all the rest of eternity*. Receive this. Turn away from self-help and sin. Become like little children. Trust him. *Trust him*. Trust him with your life.

Why Christmas Happened

> You know that he appeared in order to take away sins, and in him there is no sin. . . . The reason the Son of God appeared was to destroy the works of the devil.
>
> I JOHN 3:5, 8

Two times in 1 John 3:1–10 we are told why Christmas happened—that is, why the eternal, divine Son of God came into the world as human.

In verse 5, John says, "You know that he appeared to take away sins, and in him there is no sin." So the sinlessness of Christ is affirmed—"In him there is no sin." And the reason for his coming is affirmed—"He appeared in order to take away sins."

Then in the second part of verse 8, John says, "The reason the Son of God appeared was to destroy the works of the devil." And the specific focus John has in mind when he says "works of the devil" is the sin that the Devil promotes. We see that in the first part of verse 8: "Whoever makes a practice of sinning is of the devil, for the devil has been sinning from the beginning." So the works of the Devil that Jesus came to destroy are the works of sin.

So two times John tells us that Christmas happened—the Son of God became human—to take away sin, or to destroy the works of the Devil, namely, sin. Jesus was born of a virgin by the Holy Spirit (Matt. 1:18–20) and "increased in wisdom and in stature and in favor with God and man" (Luke 2:52) and was perfectly obedient and sinless in all his life and ministry, all the way to the point of death, even death on a cross (Phil. 2:5–8; Heb. 4:15)—in order to destroy the works of the Devil—to take away sin.

Our sin. Make this personal and love him for it. Take the very personal words of the apostle Paul and make them your own. "The life I now live in the flesh I live by faith in the Son of God, who loved me and gave himself for me" (Gal. 2:20). This is how he destroyed the works of the Devil and rescued us from our sin. Don't leave Christmas in the abstract. Your sin. Your conflict with the Devil. Your victory. He came for this.

God's Passion for God at Christmas

For this purpose I have come to this hour. Father, glorify your name.

JOHN 12:27–28

One of the most famous Christmas scenes in the Bible is the announcement to the shepherds by an angel that the Savior is born. And then it says, "Suddenly there was with the angel a multitude of the heavenly host praising God and saying, 'Glory to God in the highest, and on earth peace among those with whom he is pleased!'" (Luke 2:11–14).

Glory to God, peace to man. The angels are sent to make something crystal clear: the Son of God has come into his creation to display the glory of God and to reconcile people from alienation to peace with God. *To make God look great in salvation and to make man glad in God.*

So when we come to John 12, there is no surprise when we hear Jesus praying that this would actually happen at the most important point of his earthly life, namely, his death and resurrection. That God would in fact be glorified in the rescue of sinners. Look at John 12:27–30:

> "Now is my soul troubled. And what shall I say? 'Father, save me from this hour'? [We know he means the hour of his death, because in verse 24 he had said, "Unless a grain of wheat falls into the earth and dies, it remains alone; but if it dies, it bears much fruit."] But for this purpose I have come to this hour. Father, glorify your name." Then a voice came from heaven: "I have glorified it, and I will glorify it again." The crowd that stood there and heard it said that it had thundered. Others said, "An angel has spoken to him." Jesus answered, "This voice has come for your sake, not mine."

In verse 27, Jesus says, "For *this purpose* I have come to this hour." What purpose? Answer: verse 28, "Father, glorify your name." *That is why my death approaches.*

The Father hears Jesus's prayer and answers, "I have glorified it, and I will glorify it again." He had just glorified his name through Jesus in the resurrection of Lazarus (John 11:4, 40), and now he will glorify it in the death and resurrection of Jesus.

And don't miss the emphasis on God's commitment to glorify God. Not only does Jesus pray for God to glorify God: "Father, glorify your name" (v. 28), but God himself says, "I have glorified my name and I will again." God sent angels to say it in Luke 2. And God himself says it in John 12:28, "I have glorified [my name], and I will glorify it again."

The deepest reason why we live for the glory of God is that God acts for the glory of God. We are passionate about God's glory because God is passionate about God's glory.

And what makes this such good news, especially in the Gospel of John, is that the glory of God is full of grace and truth. "And the Word became flesh and dwelt among us, and we have seen his glory, glory as of the only Son from the Father, full of grace and truth" (John 1:14).

The most glorious thing about God is that he is so completely, fully self-sufficient that the glory of the fullness of his being overflows in truth and grace for his creatures. He doesn't need us. And therefore in his fullness he overflows for us. Such is the grace we receive at Christmas.

He Comes to Bless Us

Moses said, "The Lord God will raise up for you a prophet like me from your brothers. You shall listen to him in whatever he tells you. And it shall be that every soul who does not listen to that prophet shall be destroyed from the people." And all the prophets who have spoken, from Samuel and those who came after him, also proclaimed these days. You are the sons of the prophets and of the covenant that God made with your fathers, saying to Abraham, "And in your offspring shall all the families of the earth be blessed." God, having raised up his servant, sent him to you first, to bless you by turning every one of you from your wickedness.

ACTS 3:22–26

What this passage teaches us is that God brought Jesus onto the scene of history to bless people. "In your offspring shall all the families of the earth be *blessed*."

God said to his Son in heaven, "The time is fulfilled; I have promised blessing; now is the time to make good on my promise; you will be my emissary of blessing; I want blessing to come to the world; I have so much to give; go now and bless my people, bless them; indeed bless all the families of the earth through them, bless them, bless them."

You can see this in verses 25 and 26 as God's blessing is mentioned twice. In verse 26, it says explicitly that God sent Jesus to the people of Israel *to bless* them. And when it says that God sent him to Israel *first*, it means that he will send the blessing on to others after that. Verse 25 makes plain that this was God's aim in the covenant he made with Abraham: "In you *all the families of the earth shall be blessed*." Blessing for the Jews and then, through them—through the Jewish Messiah— blessing for all the peoples, and that includes you.

So I say to you that God is moving toward you with blessing in this Advent season. You are in verse 25. It doesn't matter that two millennia have passed. With God, a thousand years is as a day (2 Pet. 3:8). With him, it is as though he made this promise two days ago. That's how fresh the blessing for you is today. If you will move toward him in faith, you will receive the blessing. That is what Christmas is all about—the greatest blessing.

God Can Be Trusted

Moses said, "The Lord God will raise up for you a prophet like me from your brothers. You shall listen to him in whatever he tells you. And it shall be that every soul who does not listen to that prophet shall be destroyed from the people." And all the prophets who have spoken, from Samuel and those who came after him, also proclaimed these days. You are the sons of the prophets and of the covenant that God made with your fathers, saying to Abraham, "And in your offspring shall all the families of the earth be blessed." God, having raised up his servant, sent him to you first, to bless you by turning every one of you from your wickedness.

ACTS 3:22–26

From the same passage, we now learn that part of the blessing is the demonstration of the truthfulness of God.

Peter piles up the promises. In verse 22 he says that Moses predicted the coming of a prophet like himself. In verse 24 he says that all the prophets from Samuel on down proclaimed these days—the days of Jesus. In verse 25 he says that God made a promise to Abraham about these days. The point is that when Jesus comes, he confirms the truth of all these promises. He shows that God is trustworthy; he keeps his word.

Here is the way Paul put it in Romans 15:8: "Christ became a servant to the circumcised [that is, the Jews] to show God's truthfulness, in order to confirm the promises given to the patriarchs." So there it is, stated crystal clear: Christ came to prove that God tells the truth, that God keeps his promises. Christmas means that God can be trusted.

This is part of the *blessing* that he brings—and that he offers you in this Advent season. It is a blessing because where it is forsaken, moral and spiritual life disintegrates. The foundation of moral life is God's truthfulness. A society that forsakes the centrality of the absolute truthfulness of God forsakes the foundation of truth, the foundation of morality, and the foundation of beauty.

Christmas is the reassertion of the foundation of all truth and goodness and beauty, because Christmas means: *God is truthful.*

God's truthfulness is the constant in a universe of flux. God's truthfulness is the unwavering absolute. If we forsake God's truthfulness, the anchor is up, the rudder is loose, the keel is broken, and the ship of life (political life, social life, educational life, scientific life, family life) is simply at the mercy of the wind of human wishes.

So I say it with all my heart: demonstrating the truthfulness of God is a great blessing. Give that blessing to your children. Say to the next generation again and again: God is truthful; God keeps his word; God does not lie; God can be trusted! That's one blessing of Advent. Receive it as a wonderful Christmas gift, and give it to as many people as you can.

Why the Son of Man?

Truly, truly, I say to you, you will see heaven opened, and the angels of God ascending and descending on the Son of Man.

JOHN 1:51

Why is Jesus called *the Son of Man* in verse 51 and elsewhere in the Gospels? It has everything to do with Advent.

It's not simply because he is human. It's because the figure of a "son of man" in Daniel 7:13 is both human and far more than human. This was Jesus's favorite designation for himself—*Son of Man*. It's used over eighty times in the Gospels, and only Jesus uses it to refer to himself.

He got the title "Son of Man" from Daniel 7:13–14:

I saw in the night visions,

> and behold, with the clouds of heaven
> there came one like *a son of man*,
> and he came to the Ancient of Days
> and was presented before him.

> And to him was given dominion
>   and glory and a kingdom,
> that all peoples, nations, and languages
>   should serve him;
> his dominion is an everlasting dominion,
>   which shall not pass away,
> and his kingdom one
>   that shall not be destroyed.

This is the language of kingship and glory and sovereignty (John 3:13; 5:27; 6:62). But it has a different ring than the titles *Son of God* and *King of Israel*. It sounds more lowly and ordinary. So when he used it, his claims to kingship and glory and sovereignty didn't sound so overt. Only those who had ears to hear broke through to the exalted meaning of the term *Son of Man* when Jesus used it.

So this time it was not the Jewish leaders who used the title to bring him to the cross. Jesus himself used it that way. The key verse is John 3:14–15: "As Moses lifted up the serpent in the wilderness, so must *the Son of Man* be lifted up, that whoever believes in him may have eternal life."

So you could say that the greatest glory Nathanael, or you and I, would ever see is the glory of the Son of Man, the Lord of heaven, whose dominion is an everlasting dominion, lifted up on a cross to die for sinners.

So when you see him this Advent season as *Son of God* and as *King of Israel* and as *Son of Man*, make sure that you see him dying to give you eternal life and, therefore, see him as glorious.

What Christmas Came to Destroy

The reason the Son of God appeared was to destroy the works of the devil.

1 JOHN 3:8

The coming of the eternal Son of God into the world as the God-man, Jesus Christ, is a fact of history. Yet thousands of people say they believe this fact but then live just like everybody else. They have the same anxieties that good things will be lost and the same frustrations that crummy things can't be changed. Evidently, there is not much power in giving right answers on religious surveys about historical facts.

That's because the coming of the Son of God into the world is so much more than a historical fact. It was a message of hope sent by God to teenagers and single parents and crabby husbands and sullen wives and overweight women and impotent men and disabled neighbors and people with same-sex attraction and preachers and lovers—and you.

And since the Son of God lived, died, rose, reigns, and is coming again, God's message through him is more than a historical fact. It is a Christmas gift to you from the voice of the living God.

Thus says the Lord: the meaning of Christmas is that what is good and precious in your life need never be lost, and what is evil and undesirable in your life can be changed. The fears that the few good things that make you happy are slipping through your fingers, and the frustrations that the bad things you hate about yourself or your situation can't be changed—these fears and these frustrations are what Christmas came to destroy.

It is God's message of hope this Advent that what is good need never be lost and what is bad can be changed. The Devil works to take the good and bring the bad. And Jesus came to destroy the works of the Devil.

The Celebration of God's Love

God so loved the world, that he gave his only Son, that whoever believes in him should not perish but have eternal life.

JOHN 3:16

In John 3:16, Jesus teaches us that the God who exists loves. Let that sink in. The God who absolutely is. Loves. *He loves.* Of all the things you might say about God, be sure to say this: he loves.

The same writer of John 3:16 says in 1 John 4:8, "God is love." Which I take to mean at least this: giving what's good and serving the benefit of others is closer to the essence of God than getting and being served. God *is* without needs. God inclines to meet needs. God *is* a giver. God is love.

So Jesus tells us more specifically what he means by love in John 3:16. "God so loved . . ." The "so" here doesn't mean an amount of love, but a way of loving. He doesn't mean, *God loved so much*, but *God loved this way*. "God so loved" means "God thus loved."

How? What is the way God loved? He loved such "that he gave his only Son." And we know that this giving was a giving up to rejection and death. "He came to his own, and his own people did not receive him" (John 1:11). Instead they killed him. And Jesus said of all this, "I glorified you [Father] on earth, having accomplished the work that you gave me to do" (John 17:4). So when the Father gave his only begotten Son, he gave him to die.

That's the kind of love the Father has. It is a giving love. It gives his most precious treasure—his Son.

Meditate on that this Advent. It was a very costly love. A very powerful love. A very rugged, painful love. The meaning of Christmas is the celebration of this love. "God so loved . . ." And wonder of wonders, God gives this costly love to an undeserving world of sinners, like us.

The Glory of the Word Made Flesh

In the beginning was the Word, and the Word was with God, and the Word was God.

JOHN 1:1

There have always been sectarian groups who have resisted the mystery implied in these two phrases: "the Word was with God" and "the Word was God." They say, in their bondage to merely human conceptuality, you can't have it both ways. Either he *was* God, or he was *with* God. If he was *with* God, he wasn't God. And if he *was* God, he wasn't with God.

So to escape the truth of these two sentences, sometimes they change the translation. But what this verse teaches is that the one we know as Jesus Christ, before he was made flesh, *was God*, and that the Father also was God. There are a plurality of persons and a singular God. This is part of the truth that we know as the Trinity. This is why we worship Jesus Christ and say with Thomas in John 20:28, "My Lord and my God!"

John 1:1: "In the beginning was *the Word*, and *the Word* was with God, and *the Word* was God."

Why was he called "the Word"? One way to answer this is to ponder what he might have been called and why this would have been inadequate in relationship to "the Word."

For example, he might have been called "the Deed." One of the differences between a deed and a word is that a deed is more ambiguous. If we think our *words* are sometimes unclear and subject to various interpretations, our *deeds* are far more unclear and ambiguous. That's why we so often explain ourselves with words. Words capture the meaning of what we do more clearly than the deeds themselves. God did many mighty deeds in history, but he gave a certain priority to the Word. One of the reasons, I think, is that he puts a high value on clarity and communication.

Another example is that John might have called him "the Thought." In the beginning was the Thought. But one of the differences between a thought and a word is that a word is generally pictured as moving outward from the thinker for the sake of establishing communication. I think John wanted us to conceive of the Son of God as existing both for the sake of communication between him and the Father and for the sake of appearing in history as God's communication to us.

A third example is that John might have called him "the Feeling." In the beginning was the Feeling. But again, I would say, feelings do not carry any clear conception or intention or meaning. Feelings, like deeds, are ambiguous and need to be explained—with words.

So it seems to me that calling Jesus "the Word" is John's way of emphasizing that the very existence of the Son of God is for the sake of communication. First, and foremost, he exists, and has always existed, from all eternity for the sake of communication with the Father. Secondarily, but infinitely important for us, the Son of God became divine communication to us. One might say, in summary, calling Jesus "the Word" implies that he is "God-Expressing-Himself." To us.

Christmas Cut History in Half

All the prophets who have spoken, from Samuel and those who came after him, also proclaimed these days.

There is something tremendously important to get hold of here for understanding the biblical teaching about prophecy and fulfillment.

We often think of prophecy as relating to what is yet future or to what is now beginning to happen in the world. And we easily forget that what is *past* for us was *future* for the prophets.

What we need to remember is that with the coming of Jesus Christ into the world, the days of fulfillment, proclaimed by all the prophets, began. And ever since the first Christmas we have been living in those days. The "last days" foretold by the prophets are not the twenty-first century. The last days began in AD 1.

This is the uniform New Testament witness. Paul said in 1 Corinthians 10:11 that the Old Testament events happened "to them as an example, but they were written down for our instruction, on whom the end of the ages has come." For Paul, the end of the ages was not two thousand years later in the twenty-first century.

No. The beginning of the end was already present in the first century. The long-awaited Messiah had come. So the writer to the Hebrews (1:1–2) says, "At many times and in many ways, God spoke to our fathers by the prophets, but in these last days he has spoken to us by his Son." When God sent his Son into the world, the last days began.

It is a great privilege to live in the last days because, Joel prophesied, "in the last days . . . God will pour out his Spirit upon all flesh" (Joel 2:28). All the prophets looked forward to the day when the Messiah, the Son of David, the King of Israel, would come, for that would be a day of great blessing for God's people. And now he has come, his kingdom has been inaugurated, and we live in an age of fulfillment.

What we anticipate in the future at Christ's second coming is not something *completely* new but rather the consummation of the blessings we already enjoy, because the promises have begun to be fulfilled in our lives.

Christmas cut history into two ages: the age of promise and the age of fulfillment. So when Peter says in Acts 3:24, "All the prophets . . . proclaimed these days," we see that he means "these last days" (Heb. 1:2), in which God has spoken to us in his Son, the days from the first Christmas to the time of consummation yet to come.

This is where we live. The *already* of fulfillment is massive—

incarnation, crucifixion, atonement, propitiation, resurrection, ascension, heavenly reign, intercession, outpouring of the Holy Spirit, global missions, ingathering of the nations, church, New Testament Scriptures, prayer in Jesus's name, joy unspeakable, and purchased certainty.

But the *not yet* is real and wonderful and waiting for its time: the second coming, the resurrection of the dead, new and glorious bodies, the end of sinning, glorification, judgment on all unbelief, rewards, entrance into the Master's joy, new heavens and new earth, Jesus present among his people face-to-face, no more misery, pleasures forevermore.

Christmas split history. Foretastes of the future abound. Drink deeply on what he achieved for us. And be filled with hope for all that is coming.

The Mercy He Promises

I tell you that Christ became a servant to the circumcised to show God's truthfulness, in order to confirm the promises given to the patriarchs, and in order that the Gentiles might glorify God for his mercy.

ROMANS 15:8–9

God's gifts are precious beyond words, and we will sing of them forever. But the most precious gifts you can think of are not ends in themselves. They all lead to God himself. Ultimately, that is what all his gifts are for.

Take forgiveness, for example. When Christ became our servant as a ransom, he took away the curse of the law and the threat of punishment for all who believe. But to what end? That we might enjoy sin with impunity? No. That we might enjoy God for eternity! Forgiveness is precious because it brings us home to God.

Why does anyone want to be forgiven? If the answer is just for psychological relief, or just for escape from hell, or just to have more physical pleasures, then God is not honored.

Romans 15:9 says that the aim of Christ's serving us is that the Gentiles "glorify God" for his mercy. But if we exploit God's mercy as a ticket to enjoy sin—or even just to enjoy innocent things—God gets no glory from that. God gets glory for showing mercy when his mercy frees us to see him as the best gift of his mercy—as the most enjoyable person in the universe.

So it is good for us that Christ came on behalf of the truth of God, because the essence of the mercy he promised was himself.

It is good for us that Christ came on behalf of the truth of God, because his coming this way shows that God is true first and foremost to himself; and he confirms the promises of God, and that the promises are promises of mercy; and he shows that the essence of the mercy he promised is himself.

This is the meaning of his coming. This is the meaning of Christmas. Oh, that God would waken your heart to your deep need for mercy as a sinner! And then ravish your heart with a great Savior, Jesus Christ. And then release your tongue to praise him and your hands to make his mercy shine in yours.

Our Truest Treasure

When they saw the star, they rejoiced exceedingly with great joy.

MATTHEW 2:10

Worshiping Jesus means joyfully ascribing authority and dignity to Christ with sacrificial gifts. We ascribe to him. We don't add to him. God is not served by human hands as though he needed anything (Acts 17:25).

So the gifts of the magi are not given by way of assistance or need meeting. It would dishonor a monarch if foreign visitors came with royal care packages. Nor are these gifts meant to be bribes. God tells us in Deuteronomy 10:17 that he takes no bribe.

Well, what then do the gifts mean? How are they worship? The gifts are intensifiers of desire for Christ himself in much the same way that fasting is. When you give a gift to Christ like this, it's a way of saying something like this:

The joy that I pursue is not the hope of getting rich with things from you. I have not come to you for your things

> *but for yourself. And this desire I now intensify and demonstrate by giving up things in the hope of enjoying you more, not the things. By giving to you what you do not need and what I might enjoy, I am saying more earnestly and more authentically, "You are my treasure, not these things."*

I think that's what it means to worship God with gifts of gold and frankincense and myrrh.

May God take the truth of this text and waken in us a desire for Christ himself. May we say from the heart,

> *Lord Jesus, you are the Messiah, the king of Israel. All nations will come and bow down before you. God wields the world to see that you are worshiped. Therefore, whatever opposition I may find, I joyfully ascribe authority and dignity to you and bring my gifts to say that you alone can satisfy my heart, not these.*

Freed to Be Part of God's Family

The Son of Man came not to be served but to serve, and to give his life as a ransom for many.

MARK 10:45

The reason we need a ransom to be paid for us is that we have sold ourselves into sin and have been alienated from a holy God. When Jesus gave his life as a ransom, our slave masters, sin and death and the Devil, had to give up their claim on us. And the result was that we could be adopted into the family of God.

Paul put it like this in Galatians 4:4–5: "When the fullness of time had come, God sent forth his Son, born of woman, born under the law, to redeem those who were under the law, so that we might receive adoption as sons." In other words, the redemption, or the ransom, frees us to be a part of God's family. We had run away and sold ourselves into slavery. But God pays a ransom and redeems us out of slavery into the Father's house.

To do that, God's Son had to become human so that he could suffer and die in our place to pay the ransom. That is the meaning of Christmas. Hebrews 2:14 puts it like this: "Since therefore the children share in flesh and blood, he himself likewise partook of the same things, that through death he might destroy the one who has the power of death."

In other words, the reason Christ took on our full humanity was so that he could die and in dying pay a ransom and free us from the power of death. And free us to be included in his own family. The ransom is ultimately about relationship. Yours to God, your merciful Father.

He Came to Serve

Whoever would be first among you must be slave of all.

MARK 10:44

Jesus expects his disciples to be radically different from the way people ordinarily act. They are to serve each other and unbelievers. In that service they are to drink the cup of whatever suffering it will cost. And it will cost.

But if that were the only message of Christianity, it would not be good news. There would be no gospel. I need more than for someone to tell me what I should do and should be. I need help to be and to do. This is why Jesus says what he says in Mark 10:45: "The Son of Man came not to be served but to serve." What a horrendous mistake it would be if we heard Jesus's call to be the servant of all in verse 44 as a call to serve him.

It is not.

It is a call to learn how to be served by him. Don't miss this. This is the heart of Christianity. This is what sets our faith off from all other major religions. Our God does not need our service, nor is he glorified by recruits who want to help him out. Our God is so full and so self-sufficient and so overflowing in power and life and joy that he glorifies himself by serving us.

He does this by taking on humanity and seeking us out and then telling us that he did *not* come to get our service, but to be our servant.

Here is a general truth to ponder and believe: every time Jesus commands something for us to do, it is his way of telling us how he wants to serve us. Let me say it another way: the path of obedience is the place where Christ meets us as our servant to carry our burdens and give us his power.

When you become a Christian—a disciple of Jesus—you do not become his helper. He becomes your helper. You do not become his benefactor. He becomes your benefactor. You do not become his servant. He becomes your servant. Jesus does not need your help; he commands your obedience and offers his help.

Christmas. He came to serve, not to be served. He came to help us do everything he calls us to do.

Graciously and Tenderly Frustrating

God put [Christ] forward . . . to show his righteousness at the present time, so that he might be just and the justifier of the one who has faith in Jesus.

ROMANS 3:25–26

The story of Martin Luther's conversion illustrates a point. He had almost been struck with lightning and made a vow to God to become a monk. But as a monk he was utterly unable to find peace with God. He sought God in every way the church of that day taught him—in good works, in the merits of the saints, in the process of confession and absolution, in the ladder of mysticism. On top of all this, they appointed him to the university to study and teach the Bible.

Listen to the way Luther later described his breakthrough. How was he prepared to see and receive Christ for who he really is?

I greatly longed to understand Paul's Epistle to the Romans and nothing stood in the way but that one expression, "the justice of God," because I took it to mean that justice whereby God is just and deals justly in punishing the unjust. My situation was that, although an impeccable monk, I stood before God as a sinner troubled in conscience, and I had no confidence that my merit would assuage him. Therefore I did not love a just and angry God, but rather hated and murmured against him. Yet I clung to the dear Paul and had a great yearning to know what he meant.

Night and day I pondered until I saw the connection between the justice of God and the statement that "the just shall live by his faith." Then I grasped that the justice of God is that righteousness by which through grace and sheer mercy God justifies us through faith. Thereupon I felt myself to be reborn and to have gone through open doors into paradise.

In the monastery Luther had come to the end of himself. He had despaired of salvation by his own hand. But by the grace of God he did not give up his longing and his hope. He directed his attention to the one place he hoped to find help—the Bible. He said, "I greatly longed to understand." He said, "I had a great yearning" to know what it meant. And he said, "Night and day I pondered."

In other words, God prepared Luther to see the true meaning of Christ and accept it, by stirring up a deep and powerful longing in his heart for consolation and redemption that could come only from Christ.

And this is what God does again and again. He may be doing it for you in this Advent season—graciously and tenderly frustrating you with life that is not centered on Christ and filling you with longings and desires that can't find their satisfaction in what this world offers, but only in the God-man.

What a Christmas gift that might be! Let all your frustrations with this world throw you onto the Word of God. It will become sweet—like walking into paradise.

The Gift You Cannot Buy

The God who made the world and everything in it, being Lord of heaven and earth, does not live in temples made by man, nor is he served by human hands, as though he needed anything, since he himself gives to all mankind life and breath and everything.

ACTS 17:24–25

God does not want to be served in any way that implies we are supplying his need or supporting him or offering him something that he does not already own by right. "Who has given a gift to him that he might be repaid?" (Rom. 11:35). "If I were hungry, I would not tell you, for the world and its fullness are mine" (Ps. 50:12).

Therefore, we simply cannot negotiate with God. We have nothing of value that is not already his by right. We cannot service him. His car never breaks down. It never runs out of gas. It never gets dirty. He never gets tired. He never gets depressed.

He never gets caught in traffic so that he can't get to where he wants to go. He never gets lonely. He never gets hungry.

In other words, if you want what Jesus has to give, you can't buy it. You can't trade for it. You can't work for it. He already owns your money and everything you have. And when you work, it is only because he has given you life and breath and everything. All we can do is submit to his spectacular offer to be our servant.

And this submission is called faith—a willingness to let him be God. Trust him to be the Supplier, the Strengthener, the Counselor, the Guide, the Savior. And being satisfied with that—with all that God is for us in Jesus. That's what faith is. And having that is what it means to be a Christian.

Christmas means: the infinitely self-sufficient God has come not to be assisted but to be enjoyed.

Receive His Reconciliation

More than that, we also rejoice in God through our Lord Jesus Christ, through whom we have now received reconciliation.

ROMANS 5:11

How do we practically receive reconciliation and rejoice in God? Answer: *through Jesus Christ*. Which means, at least in part, make the portrait of Jesus in the Bible—the work and the words of Jesus portrayed in the New Testament—the essential content of your rejoicing in God. Rejoicing without the content of Christ does not honor Christ.

In 2 Corinthians 4:4–6, Paul describes conversion two ways. In verse 4 he says it is seeing "the glory of Christ, who is the image of God." And in verse 6 he says it is seeing "the glory of God in the face of Jesus Christ." In either case, you can see the point. We have Christ, the image of God, and we have God in the face of Christ.

Practically, to rejoice in God, you rejoice in what you see and know of God in the portrait of Jesus Christ. And this comes to its fullest experience when the love of God is poured out in our hearts by the Holy Spirit (Rom. 5:5).

Not only did God purchase our reconciliation through the death of our Lord Jesus Christ (Rom. 5:10), and not only did God enable us to receive that reconciliation through our Lord Jesus Christ, but even now we exult in God himself through our Lord Jesus Christ.

Jesus purchased our reconciliation. Jesus enabled us to receive the reconciliation and open the gift. And Jesus himself shines forth from the wrapping—the indescribable gift—as God in the flesh, and stirs up all our rejoicing in God.

Look to Jesus this Christmas. Receive the reconciliation that he bought. Don't put it on the shelf unopened. And don't open it and then make it a means to all your other pleasures. Open it and enjoy the gift. Rejoice in him. Make him your pleasure. Make him your treasure.

Get Your Eyes Ready for Christmas

He said to them, "But who do you say that I am?"
Simon Peter replied, "You are the Christ, the Son of the
living God." And Jesus answered him, "Blessed are you,
Simon Bar-jonah! For flesh and blood has not revealed
this to you, but my Father who is in heaven."

MATTHEW 16:15–17

The absolutely indispensable work of God in revealing the
Son—both then to Peter and now to you and me—is not the
adding to what we see and hear in Jesus himself but the opening of the eyes of our hearts to taste and see the true divine
glory of what is really there in Jesus.

When people have doubts about the truth of Jesus, don't
send them away to seek special messages from God. Point
them to Christ. Tell them what you have seen and heard in
his life and teachings. Why? Because this is where God breaks
in with his revealing power. He loves to glorify his *Son*! He

loves to open the eyes of the blind when they are looking at his *Son*!

God does not reveal his Son to me by coming to me and saying, "Now, John, I know that you don't see anything magnificent in my Son. You don't see him as all glorious and divine and attractive above all worldly goods. You don't see him as your all-satisfying treasure, and you don't see his holiness and wisdom and power and love as beautiful beyond measure. But take my word for it, he is all that. Just believe it." *No!*

Such faith would be no honor to the Son of God. It cannot glorify the Son. Saving faith is based on a spiritual sight of Jesus as he is in himself, the all-glorious Son of God. And this spiritual sight is given to us through his inspired Word, the Scriptures. And the eyes of our hearts are opened to recognize him and receive him not by the wisdom of flesh and blood but by the revealing work of his heavenly Father.

The apostle Paul said, "God, who said, 'Let light shine out of darkness,' has shone in our hearts to give the light of the knowledge of the glory of God in the face of Jesus Christ."

How shall you prepare your heart this Christmas to receive Christ? Fix your gaze on him in the Bible. Look to Christ! Consider Jesus. And pray. Look beyond your own flesh and blood, and ask that God would give you eyes to see and ears to hear that you might cry out with Peter, "You are the Christ the Son of the living God!"

Something Worth Singing About

There are priests who offer gifts according to the law. They serve a copy and shadow of the heavenly things. . . . Christ has obtained a ministry that is as much more excellent than the old as the covenant he mediates is better, since it is enacted on better promises. . . .

"This is the covenant that I will make . . .
I will put my laws into their minds,
    and write them on their hearts,
and I will be their God,
    and they shall be my people."

HEBREWS 8:4–10

Here we see that Christmas means two things. First, it means the replacement of Old Testament shadows with reality. The temple and sacrifices and priesthood and feasts and dietary laws were all shadows and copies of the reality in heaven. That reality is Jesus Christ and his work as our High Priest and our sacrifice and our focus of worship. Jesus fulfills and replaces the shadows of the Old Testament.

Second, it means that God makes the reality of Christ real to us personally by the work of the new covenant when he writes his truth on our hearts. God moves powerfully into our hearts and minds to overcome our resistance to the beauty of his reality. He writes his will—the truth of the reality of Jesus—on our hearts, so that we see him for who he really is and are willing and eager to trust him and follow him— freely, from the inside out, not slavishly under constraint from outside.

God is just and holy and separated from sinners—sinners like you and me. This is our main problem at Christmas—and every other season. *How shall we be put right with a just and holy God?* Nevertheless, God is merciful and promised in Jeremiah 31 (five hundred years before Christ came) that someday he would do something new. He would replace shadows with the reality of the Messiah. And he would powerfully move into our lives and write his will on our hearts so that we are not constrained from the outside but are willing from the inside— to love him and trust him and follow him.

That would be the greatest salvation imaginable—if God should offer us the greatest reality in the universe to enjoy and then move in us to see to it that we could enjoy it with the greatest freedom and the greatest pleasure possible. That would be a Christmas gift worth singing about. And that is exactly what he has done.

Our Deepest Need at Christmas

He shall stand and shepherd his flock in the strength of
    the LORD,
  in the majesty of the name of the LORD his God.
And they shall dwell secure, for now he shall be great
    to the ends of the earth.
And he shall be their peace.

MICAH 5:4–5

"He shall be great to the ends of the earth," Micah prophesies. There will be no pockets of resistance unsubdued. Our security will not be threatened by any alien forces. Every knee will bow and every tongue will confess him Lord. The whole earth will be filled with his glory.

And "he will be our peace." Yes, in this context that includes final, earthly, political peace. Micah spoke of it already in Micah 4:3:

> He shall judge between many peoples,
>> and shall decide for strong nations far away;
> and they shall beat their swords into plowshares,
>> and their spears into pruning hooks;
> nation shall not lift up sword against nation,
>> neither shall they learn war anymore.

One day the ruler—the King of kings and Lord of lords—will return and make that a reality. The great Christmas carol will finally be fulfilled:

> He rules the world with truth and grace
> And makes the nations prove
> The glories of his righteousness
> And wonders of his love.

But there is another, deeper peace—a peace that must happen before there can be peace on earth. There must be peace between us and God. Our unbelief and his wrath must be removed. That is our deepest peace—and our deepest need at Christmas.

Micah knew it was coming. He had experienced it personally (Mic. 7:8–9). He describes it beautifully at the very end of his book, in Micah 7:18–19:

> Who is a God like you, pardoning iniquity
>> and passing over transgression
>> for the remnant of his inheritance?
> He does not retain his anger forever,
>> because he delights in steadfast love.

He will again have compassion on us;
> he will tread our iniquities underfoot.
You will cast all our sins
> into the depths of the sea.

This was the great work of the Messiah yet to be done. Yes, there are enemies on earth that must be defeated if we are to have peace. But, oh, the great enemy called sin and judgment—that is the greatest and worst enemy. The gospel at Christmas is: *Christ has trampled this enemy underfoot at the cross. So for everyone who trusts in him, their sins are cast into the depths of the sea.*

Therefore, we say not, "Glory to us," but, "Glory to God in the highest, and on earth peace among those with whom he is pleased!"

Enjoy All the Promises of God

But you, O Bethlehem Ephrathah,
    who are too little to be among the clans of Judah,
from you shall come forth for me
    one who is to be ruler in Israel,
whose coming forth is from of old,
    from ancient days.
Therefore he shall give them up until the time
    when she who is in labor has given birth;
then the rest of his brothers shall return
    to the people of Israel.
And he shall stand and shepherd his flock in the strength
      of the LORD,
    in the majesty of the name of the LORD his God.

MICAH 5:2–4

Christ is the yes of all God's promises, so if you trust him, they will all be your inheritance. Already Micah made clear that Christ will secure for us the promises of God. How did Micah show us this?

Any Jewish person in those days, hearing Micah predict the coming of a ruler out of Bethlehem who would feed his flock in the strength of the Lord, would think immediately of two people: David the king and the coming Son of David, the Messiah.

There are at least three links with David in this text: (1) David was from Bethlehem—that's why it was called the "city of David." (2) David was a ruler in Israel—he was the greatest ruler, a man after God's own heart. (3) David was a shepherd as a boy, and later he was called the shepherd of Israel (Ps. 78:71).

The point of these three links with David is this: Micah is reasserting the certainty of God's promise to David. Recall from 2 Samuel 7:12–16 that God said to David,

> I will raise up your offspring after you, who shall come from your body and I will establish his kingdom. He shall build a house for my name, and I will establish the throne of his kingdom forever. . . . And your house and your kingdom shall be made sure forever before me. Your throne shall be established forever.

The amazing thing about Micah is that he reasserts the certainty of this promise not at a time when Israel is rising to power but at a time when Israel is sinking toward oblivion. The northern kingdom is destroyed, and the southern kingdom will come under the judgment of God. The promises of God looked impossible.

Micah's point was this: *the coming of Christ was the confirmation of the promises of God*. Here's the way Paul put it in Romans 15:8: "Christ became a servant to the circumcised to show God's truthfulness, in order to confirm the promises given to the patriarchs." Or as he said in 2 Corinthians 1:20, "All the promises of God find their Yes in him."

If you are "in him" by faith, you will inherit all the promises of God. Micah's prediction came true in Jesus. And thus all the promises were confirmed. God has told the truth. Christmas is God's great confirmation of all his promises. If Christ has come, God is true. And if God is true, all the promises will come true for all who trust him. Receive this unspeakable gift.

Grace: The Dominant Note of Christmas

I am the living bread that came down from heaven. If anyone eats of this bread, he will live forever. And the bread that I will give for the life of the world is my flesh.

JOHN 6:51

There is no traditional Christmas story about the birth of Jesus in the Gospel of John. You remember how it begins: "In the beginning was the Word, and the Word was with God, and the Word was God" (John 1:1). Instead of putting the Christmas story up front with its explanation, John weaves the story of Christmas and the purpose of Christmas through the Gospel.

For example, after saying that the Word "was God," John says, "And the Word became flesh and dwelt among us, and we have seen his glory, glory as of the only Son from the Father, full of grace and truth. . . . And from his fullness we have all received, grace upon grace" (John 1:14–16).

So the eternal Word of God took on human flesh, and in

that way the divine Son of God—who never had an origin, and never came into being, and *was* God, but was also *with* God—became man. And in doing this, he made the glory of God visible in a wholly new way. And this divine glory, uniquely manifest in the Son of God, was full of grace and truth. And from that fullness we receive grace upon grace.

That is the meaning of Christmas in John's Gospel. God the Son, who *is* God, and who is *with* God, came to reveal God in a way he had never been revealed before. And in that revelation, the dominant note struck is grace: from the fullness of that revelation of divine glory, we receive grace upon grace.

Or as it says in John 3:16–17, "God so loved the world, that he gave his only Son, [that's Christmas and Good Friday all in one] that whoever believes in him should not perish but have eternal life. For God did not send his Son into the world to condemn the world [Christmas is not for condemnation], but in order that the world might be saved through him [Christmas is for salvation]."

And at the end of his life, Jesus was standing before Pilate, and Pilate said to him, "So you are a king?" And Jesus answered, "You say that I am a king. For this purpose I was born and for this purpose I have come into the world [this is the purpose of Christmas]—to bear witness to the truth. Everyone who is of the truth listens to my voice" (John 18:37).

What was the effect of the truth that Jesus witnessed to with his words and his whole person? He told us in John 8:31–32, "If you abide in my word, you are truly my disciples, and you will know the truth, and the truth will set you free." So the meaning of Christmas is this: the Son of God came into the world to bear witness to the truth in a way that it had never been witnessed to before.

He *is* the way, the *truth*, and the life (John 14:6). And the aim of giving himself as the truth to the world is *freedom*. You will know the truth, and the truth will make you *free*. Free from the guilt and power of sin. Free from deadness and blindness and judgment.

How does that liberation happen? Recall from John 6 that in coming down from heaven, Jesus was planning to die. He came to die. He came to live a perfect, sinless life and then die for sinners. John 6:51: "I am the living bread that came down from heaven. If anyone eats of this bread, he will live forever. And the bread that I will give for the life of the world is my flesh."

The Word became flesh and dwelt among us, so that he could give his flesh for the life of the world. We sinners can receive grace upon grace from his fullness because he came to die for us. Christmas was from the beginning a preparation for Good Friday.

So throughout the Gospel of John the meaning of Christmas becomes clear. The Word became flesh. He revealed the glory of God as never before. He died according to his own plan. Because of his death in our place, he is bread for us. He is the source of forgiveness and righteousness and life. This is the great meaning of Christmas in the Gospel of John. Indeed in the world. Today.

A Savior Is Born! God Gets the Glory, You Get the Peace

A Christmas Sermon

Some of the most familiar and happy words of Christmas are these:

> For unto you is born this day in the city of David a Savior, who is Christ the Lord. And this will be a sign for you: you will find a baby wrapped in swaddling cloths and lying in a manger." And suddenly there was with the angel a multitude of the heavenly host praising God and saying,
>
> > "Glory to God in the highest,
> > and on earth peace among those with whom he is pleased!" (Luke 2:11–14)

Let's exult together over the wonders in this text. On our way to the glory and the peace of verse 14 there are wonders to see.

"*For unto you is born this day . . .*" It happened on a day. A day in history. Not a day in some mythological, imaginary story, but a day when Caesar Augustus was the emperor of Rome "and Quirinius was governor of Syria" (v. 2).

It was a day planned in eternity before the creation of the world. Indeed the whole universe—with untold light-years of space and billions of galaxies—was created and made glorious for this day and what it means for human history.

> For by him all things were created, in heaven and on earth, visible and invisible, whether thrones or dominions or rulers or authorities—all things were created through him and *for him*. (Col. 1:16)

For him! For his appearance. For this day of his appearing. "When the fullness of time had come, God sent forth his Son, born of woman, born under the law" (Gal. 4:4). It happened on a day. The perfect day. In the fullness of time. The perfect time appointed by God before the foundation of the world. "For unto you is born *this day*!"

". . . *in the city of David . . .*" It happened in a city. Not in Narnia. Not in Middle Earth. Not in a galaxy far, far away. It happened in a city about seven thousand miles from Minneapolis. The city still exists today. My mother was killed in a bus accident just outside this city. This city is real.

The city's name is Bethlehem (Luke 2:4, "Joseph also went up from Galilee . . . to the city of David, which is called Bethlehem.") Bethlehem, six miles from Jerusalem. Bethlehem, the city where Jesse lived, the father of David, the great king of Israel. Bethlehem, the city that Micah prophesied over:

> But you, O Bethlehem Ephrathah,
>> who are too little to be among the clans of Judah,
> from you shall come forth for me
>> one who is to be ruler in Israel,
> whose coming forth is from of old,
>> from ancient days. (Mic. 5:2)

It happened in a city. A real city, like the city you live in.

Savior, Messiah, Lord

". . . *a Savior* . . ." "For unto you is born this day in the city of David *a Savior*." A Savior. If you have ever sinned against God, you need a Savior. The angel said to Joseph, "You shall call his name Jesus, for he will save his people from their sins" (Matt. 1:21). Only God can forgive sins against God. That is why God sent the eternal Son of God into the world, because he is God. That's why Jesus said, "The Son of Man has authority on earth to forgive sins." Therefore, a Savior was born.

". . . *who is Christ* . . ." "For unto you is born this day in the city of David a Savior, *who is Christ*." *Christ* is the English for *Christos*, which means "anointed one," which is the meaning of "Messiah" (John 1:41; 4:25). This is the one long-predicted, long-awaited, the one anointed above all others (Ps. 45:7). The final anointed king. The final anointed prophet. The final anointed priest. In him all the promises of God are yes! (2 Cor. 1:20). He would fulfill all the hopes and dreams of godly Israel. And more, vastly more. Because he is also . . .

". . . *the Lord.*" "For unto you is born this day in the city of David a Savior, who is Christ *the Lord.*" The ruler, the sovereign, the mighty God, the everlasting Father. The Lord of the universe.

> For to us a child is born,
>   to us a son is given;
> and the government shall be upon his shoulder,
>   and his name shall be called
> Wonderful Counselor, Mighty God,
>   Everlasting Father, Prince of Peace.
> Of the increase of his government and of peace
>   there will be no end. (Isa. 9:6–7)

Christmas in Sum

The Lord of never-ending, universal, sovereign governance. The Lord of all lords.

- On a day—in real history.
- In a city—in a real world.
- The Savior—to take away all our guilt.
- The Christ—to fulfill all our hopes.
- The Lord—to defeat all our enemies and make us safe and satisfied for ever.

So I exult with you this Christmas that we have a great Savior, Jesus, the Christ, the Lord, born on a day in a city to save us from our sins—our many sins.

Two Great Purposes for This Great News

And when the angel had announced this news to the shepherds (Luke 2:11) and pointed them to the very animal shed where the baby lay, suddenly an army of angels appeared in the sky. Evidently, one angel can bring the news, but it does not suffice for one angel to *respond* to the news. The *meaning* of this news, the *ultimate outcome* of this news—that demands an army of angels.

> And suddenly there was with the angel a multitude of the heavenly host [army!] praising God and saying,
>
> "Glory to God in the highest,
>> and on earth peace among those with whom he is
>> pleased!" (vv. 2:13–14)

The joyful news that on a day, at the perfect fullness of time, in the perfect prophesied city, a Savior was born, who was Christ, the Lord—that news has two great outcomes. Two great purposes. "Glory to God in the highest, and on earth peace among those with whom he is pleased!"

God's Glory and Our Peace

The coming of this child will be the greatest revelation of the glory of God even among the heights of heaven, and the coming of this child will bring peace to God's people—who will one day fill the whole earth with righteousness and peace. "Of the increase of his government *and of peace* there will be no end" (Isa. 9:7).

First and foremost, *God is glorified* because this child is born. And, second, *peace is to spread* everywhere this child is received. These are the great purposes for the coming of Jesus: glory ever ascending from man to God. Peace ever descending from God to man. God's glory sung out among men for the sake of his name. God's peace lived out among men for the sake of his name.

There is hardly a better way to sum up what God was about when he created the world, or when he came to re-claim the world in Jesus Christ—his glory, our peace. His greatness, our joy. His beauty, our pleasure. The point of creation and redemption is that God is glorious and means to be known and praised for his glory by a peace-filled new humanity.

To Experience the Peace He Brings

"Glory to God in the highest, and on earth peace among those with whom he is pleased!" The old King James Version trans-lated verse 14b, "and on earth peace, good will toward men." Virtually all the modern translations agree that this was not an accurate translation. The NIV says, ". . . and on earth peace to men *on whom his favor rests*." The NASB says, ". . . and on earth peace among *men with whom he is pleased*." And the ESV says, ". . . and on earth peace among those with whom he is pleased!"

The point is that even though God's offer of peace goes out to all, only his chosen people—the people who receive Christ and trust him as Savior and Messiah and Lord, will experience the peace he brings.

You get a glimpse of this meaning in Luke 10:5–6, where Jesus says to his disciples, "Whatever house you enter, first say, 'Peace be to this house!' [that's the offer of peace to all] And if a *son of peace* is there, your peace will rest upon him. But if not, it will return to you."

God's peace in Christ is offered to the world. But only the "sons of peace" receive it. How do you know if you are a "son of peace"? How do you know if you are part of the angels' promise, "Peace among those with whom he is pleased!"? Answer: you welcome the Peacemaker; you receive Jesus.

The Main Point of Peace

God's purpose is to give you peace by being the most glorious person in your life. Five times in the New Testament he is called "the God of peace" (Rom. 15:33; 16:20; Phil. 4:9; 1 Thess. 5:23; Heb. 13:20). And Jesus said, "My peace I give to you" (John 14:27). And Paul said, "[Jesus] himself is our peace" (Eph. 2:14).

What this means is that the peace of God, or the peace of Christ, can never be separated from God himself and Christ himself. If we want peace to rule in our lives, God must rule in our lives. Christ must rule in our lives. God's purpose is not to give you peace separate from himself. His purpose is to give you peace by being the most glorious person in your life.

So the key to peace is keeping together what the angels

keep together: glory to God and peace to man. A heart bent on showing the glory of God will know the peace of God.

And what holds the two together—God getting glory and we getting peace—is believing or trusting the promises of God obtained by Jesus. Romans 15:13 is one of those fundamental texts pointing to this crucial role of faith: "May the God of hope fill you with all joy and *peace in believing.*" In believing. In other words, the way God's promises become real for us and produce peace in us and through us is "in believing." *When we believe them.* That's true whether we are talking about peace with God, peace with ourselves, or peace with others.

Three Relationships of Peace

My great desire for you this Christmas is that you enjoy this peace. We know that there are global aspects to this peace that lie in the future when "the earth will be filled with the knowledge of the glory of the LORD as the waters cover the sea" (Hab. 2:14). When, as Isaiah says, "Of the increase of his government and of peace there will be no end" (Isa. 9:7).

But Jesus has come to inaugurate that peace among God's people. And there are three relationships in which he wants you to pursue this peace and enjoy this peace. Peace with God. Peace with your own soul. And peace with other people, as much as it lies in you.

And by peace, I mean not only the absence of conflict and animosity but also the presence of joyful tranquility, and as much richness of interpersonal communication as you are capable of.

So let's look at each of these three peaceful relationships briefly and make sure you are enjoying as much as you can. The key to each of them is not to separate what the angels kept together: the glory of God and the peace you long for. "Glory to God in the highest and on earth peace."

Peace with God

The most basic need we have is peace with God. This is foundational to all our pursuits of peace. If we don't go here first, all other experiences of peace will be superficial and temporary.

The key passage here is Romans 5:1: "Therefore, since we have been justified by faith [there's the pivotal act of believing], we have peace with God through our Lord Jesus Christ." "Justified" means that God declares you to be just in his sight by imputing to you the righteousness of Jesus.

And he does that by faith alone: "Since we have been justified *by faith*" (Rom. 5:1). Not by works. Not by tradition. Not by baptism. Not by church membership. Not by piety. Not by parentage. But by faith alone. When we believe in Jesus as the Savior and the Lord and the supreme treasure of our lives, we are united to him and his righteousness is counted by God as ours. We are justified by faith.

And the result is peace with God. God's anger at us because of our sin is put away. Our rebellion against him is overcome. God adopts us into his family. And from now on all his dealings with us are for our good. He will never be against us. He is our Father and our friend. We have peace. We don't need to be afraid any more. This is foundational to all other peace.

Peace with Ourselves

And because we have peace with God because of being justified by faith, we can begin to grow in the enjoyment of peace with ourselves—and here I include any sense of guilt or anxiety that tends to paralyze us or make us hopeless. Here again, believing the promises of God with a view to glorifying God in our lives is key.

Philippians 4:6–7 is one of the most precious passages in this regard: "Do not be anxious about anything [the opposite of anxiety is peace], but in everything by prayer and supplication with thanksgiving let your requests be made known to God [in other words, roll your anxieties onto God]. And the *peace of God*, which surpasses all understanding, will guard your hearts and your minds in Christ Jesus."

The picture here is that our hearts and our minds are under assault. Guilt, worries, threats, confusions, uncertainties— they all threaten our peace. And Paul says that God wants to "guard" our hearts and minds. He guards them with his peace. He guards them in a way that goes beyond what human understanding can fathom—"which surpasses all understanding."

Don't limit the peace of God by what your understanding can see. He gives us inexplicable peace, supra-rational peace. And he does it when we take our anxieties to him in prayer and trust him that he will carry them for us (1 Pet. 5:7) and protect us.

When we do this, when we come to him—and remember we *already* have peace with him!—and trust him as our loving and almighty Heavenly Father to help us, his peace comes to us and steadies us and protects us from the disabling effects of fear and anxiety and guilt. And then we are able to carry on, and our God gets the glory for what we do because we trusted him.

Do that this Christmas. Take your anxieties to God. Tell him about them. Ask him to help you. To protect you. To restore your peace. And then to use you to make peace.

Peace with Others

The third relationship in which God wants us to enjoy his peace is in our relationships with other people. This is the one we have least control over. So we need to say it carefully the way Paul does in Romans 12:18. He says, "If possible, so far as it depends on you, live peaceably with all."

For many of you, when you get together with family for Christmas, there will be some awkward and painful relationships. Some of the pain is very old. And some of it is new. In some relationships you know what you have to do, no matter how hard it is. And in some of them you are baffled and don't know what the path of peace calls for.

In both cases the key is trusting the promises of God with heartfelt awareness of how he forgave you through Christ. I think the text that puts this together most powerfully for me again and again is Ephesians 4:31–32: "Let all bitterness and wrath and anger and clamor and slander be put away from you, along with all malice. Be kind to one another, tender-hearted, forgiving one another, as God in Christ forgave you."

Continually cultivate a sense of amazement that in spite of all your sins, God has forgiven you through Christ. Be amazed that you have peace with God. It's this sense of amazement, that I, a sinner, have peace with God, that makes the heart tender, kind, and forgiving. Extend this to others seventy times seven.

It may be thrown back in your face. It certainly was thrown back in Jesus's face on the cross. That hurts, and it can make you bitter if you are not careful. Don't let it. Keep being more amazed that your wrongs are forgiven than that you are wronged. Be amazed that you have peace with God. You have peace with your soul. Your guilt is taken away.

Keep trusting God. He knows what he is doing. Keep his glory—not your success or your effectiveness in peacemaking or your relationships—supreme in the treasure chest of your heart.

And then you will be like the angels: glory to God in the highest is the first thing. Peace among his people is the second thing.

"For unto you is born this day in the city of David a Savior, who is Christ the Lord." This is why he came—on a day, to a city, as the Savior, Messiah, and Sovereign. That God would get glory and that you would know peace. May the God of peace give you peace and get his glory.

A Word of Thanks

Most of these devotional readings I prepared as sermons for the church I served or as devotionals for the readers of desiringGod.org. David Mathis, executive editor of Desiring God, with help from Jonathan Parnell and Tony Reinke, chose them for inclusion here and condensed them for this format. Then I read through them again and made final changes. I am deeply thankful for David's initiative and for the excellence of his work. This book would not exist without him. If there are errors or infelicities, they are owing to my oversight.

I am thankful for the entire content team at Desiring God (David, Jonathan, and Tony, with Stefan Green and Marshall Segal). Not only do they help harvest things that I have written over the years and make them available in fresh ways, but they produce content themselves which keeps the blog at desiringGod.org alive and useful. I am privileged to have such remarkably gifted partners.

All of us declare our absolute dependence of the grace of God in Christ for every breath we take, and every thought we have, and every affection we feel, and every word we write.

We are happy to be debtors to grace. Our aim is to serve in the strength that God supplies so that in everything God may get the glory through Jesus Christ. To him be the dominion forever. Amen (1 Pet. 4:11).

—John Piper

❉ desiringGod

If you would like to explore further the vision of God and life presented in this book, we at Desiring God would love to serve you. We have thousands of resources to help you grow in your passion for Jesus Christ and help you spread that passion to others. At desiringGod.org, you'll find almost everything John Piper has written and preached, including more than sixty books. We've made over thirty years of his sermons available free online for you to read, listen to, download, and watch.

In addition, you can access hundreds of articles, find out where John Piper is speaking, and learn about our conferences. Desiring God has a whatever-you-can-afford policy, designed for individuals with limited discretionary funds. If you'd like more information about this policy, please contact us at the address or phone number below. We exist to help you treasure Jesus and his gospel above all things because *he is most glorified in you when you are most satisfied in him.* Let us know how we can serve you!

Desiring God

Post Office Box 2901 / Minneapolis, Minnesota 55402
888.346.4700   mail@desiringGod.org

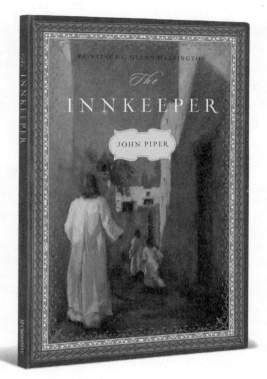

John Piper's Classic Christmas Poem

The classic poem about the innkeeper who provided the stable for Jesus's birth has been redesigned. This beautiful book will help you celebrate Christ's birth and the power of his death and resurrection.
